QUALIA PARALLAXIS

Poems

CODY GRINSLADE

First Edition

Fulton Books
Meadville, PA

Published by Fulton Books 2024

This book is a work of fiction. Names, characters, places and incidents are either the product of the author's imagination or used fictitiously.

Any resemblance to actual events or locals or persons, living or dead, is entirely coincidental.

ISBN 979-8-88982-887-7 (paperback)
ISBN 979-8-88982-888-4 (digital)

Printed in the United States of America

For Mattio, my twin brother,
because… you know why.

CONTENTS

THE NAMELESS THEME

Scrawled out nameless, naked and new
Once you have stepped through
ignivomous mountains of corpses and crowns

Where have you gone to,
when there are none left to forget?
This place is but the game

Mystics in the gardens
The limestone beast
in the eye of the Ouroboros Fountain

Blanket of empty nests
Existence—exiled mutation

Life is exactly what we're sinking in
Affective upon arrival, expectancy undeniable

The sentence is carried
The truth is then buried
No one will ever know

And from this time less consuming,
I will send them a sovereign signal
From Epoché to Ataraxia
Stinging thirst allures
Isolation—monstrous mutiny

New life of rising circumstances
feeding the daughters of mania
Devils teething over seeds
One whose love is such to die of

Horizons beneath a light that always reigns
far too late on a three moon night

The heavens full to delectable size
Never-ending wealth of life's
undying promises fall faster

Higher than any heaven could reach
If only one could break through,
we would all see it in you

SLEIGHT OF TONGUE

This is what I am worth
upon powerless hearth

One with this light
under the prowess of rebirth

I lurched and found perched,
your eye on the pride

Turning eagle to stone
Kindling your blood in the fire

The pain in the window,
webbed closed, half eaten
Left out in the open, a wounded shell

Who let these centaurs out of their celluloid?
Block all the jailbreaks
Cut 'em off at the mile
Burn the lot at the stake

There is no return of the fabled,
Toads of Cloven Smoke at Napalm Swamp

The writer writes what I see,
not what he is looking at directly

We are all ancient in this well
Careful with that eye, Horus,
it's impolite to stare

Lost in the night
My shadow friend,
found in a light

Sailing toward the beast,
the last remaining piece of you,
fading out of sight

A DEATH STORY

In the warmth of mortal hands, bleed
deeper than beyond those avoided,
before believing passion's acreage

Where ones chosen virtues
will be tired of being tested
by tried and true messages of flies

Ride that stream of screams
to the dark depths of Hades

Find that light, cherish that angel
though it no longer has its wings

Once you're down there,
down in that feeling, well—
there's no getting out without it
because it pulls you from that black, abysmal holiness
Let the demon shine as shone in your reflection

I'm coming to you somehow,
my candle in the arms of grace

I'm coming to life, my light in the dark ahead
To sing is to bleed from the halo down

I hurt, I have hurt, I still remember

Always in the air to remind me you're still here

and they're there while their idle bones
go unturned in snake years

An abundance of frailty
in the most desperate of need

Zechariel, come mend our broken child
O Cassiel, command thy speed
Berlin, sundown dawning lowly

TO WALK THIS EARTH (WITH MY OWN TWO MINDS)

How I choose to walk this Earth
Tanks giving gasoline cravings

Full of the shores of afterbirth-blue
Tentacular plague in my wounds at night
Dawn break won't guide you here

Sing for me now in your way
Emerald lungs of unknown pistol piece
Let us explore your cabinet

The snake in your eye won't save your tail
Let it go or become the veiled shadow

You've got a hard life to give
A star gone too far
Won't be long before I come back around
to find some dust to blast my mind, alas

Walked in sanity-free, clinically, then it hit me,
I can walk right out of my own painting,
out of time, out of nothing, into you
Seeing angels where evildoers dwell
What the devil's got you
doing to your self-awareness

It takes the hyacinth flower,
saws the madrigal in half the time it takes
to make a moment infinite

I hope your dream makes you turn
Toys on the floor can't close their eyes
When the dream is over, they're all that's left to
behold of you

Song for a sobriquet blue bear rhythm dissection
I've emerged from the fire you started

To end its existence—axe it, tax it, vex it
Genius response to the fool's itch

What a bloody miracle, yet for whatever crystal
reason, you never could ask for help

For the woman with the long, dark hair
and bellowing trench coat, there is no plausible way

Don't despair, this place not safe
from all that dwell into solitude
of the perplexing moment

Here is where it all ends
This is where it began to follow you
like a shadow not your own

Some place south of true north
This end, I can't see the eye anymore
Time has taken you away

The hurt has begun to stagnate
withholding the inside man of the hourglass

Blind minds see an empathetic waste
in the not-so-lonely loners pieces
Do you see them?

THESE DREAMING OF THINGS

Clear waters catch upon a burning flower
This wind's brought no such
mortal dust to hush her

This mountain's
the only beast
I have built in this filth

This monster's
the only one dreaming
I have now to keep warm

These things are as
wild as you see them
This fire's freeing me

SPINAL TAPESTRY

Around every dark corner lurks a hook, a snake, and
a cold chill up your spine
Fear of death, a stage
An ancient state of curiosity
that breaks the spirit
or sets it free from form

Hanging yawns at shut-eye burn
Turns a bloodless churning to dusk

Hold tight, midnight sage
Gleaming dark side is dawning

IN THE SNOW

We must reap it sown
In the snow

We must go
In the end

We must find it a host
In the snow
We mustn't go it alone

In the end
We must go

In the snow
We must keep it unbeknownst

SACRED EARTH SHAKER

At home on the edge of this prison's shell
Well ready to fly, yet not so steady

You said I could drop by anytime,
echoing your inner-prism cells

Always known the way back
What is your life now that
you've got a sense of direction?

Welcome to home, protector of all that's left of us
in the cities panting of the dead mélange

Tremble not your hand fed through the mindfuck
machine

This painstaking metacyanide is just warping your
head

"Here is the mind…"
Don't you go and kill 'er, Sleeper

Not in this house, traitorous,
worth its weight in emptiness and further still

Ancient worming spice works
of otherworldly essences

A dance of skulls to illuminate
all the red ruins in her riches
Danger focused to acts of kindness

In an old wedding dress,
golding locks of despair,
flared and infinite

My brother from another spider,
you will be my strength
cut from the cloth

Been there but never seen
I'll be your eyes,
your invisible tormentors

That branch had seen its better days
but it's still funny when we reminisce

"You squids come down from there!" she'd say.
Not before the sun would upset to never sleep

He's come to tear us out,
to steep us into nowhere
on gifted wings

A blessing that keeps its curtains closed
Midnight curses always baying

at the banter of the old guardianships
Empath, prepare for impact

Born in winter of spring's song
Couldn't have been for
anyone else but her darkest

and as the cradle rocks
your world to sleep,

your soul may flower
every time you look up on high

It's deep inside of your self
Look toward death before afterlife
No answer as to why or how long ago

KNOW THYSELF FOOL

One too many divided between me and mercy,
infinity finds us incessantly
inventing new words left for use

Tell me once more
Don't tell me you knew

Now too late to call for help
Was it all for nothing?

Then shines the brightest of bulbs
I almost felt sorry for the poor bastard

For what do you wander, and what do you carry?

Whom shall I bury next?
How do you ever expect to learn?

I don't want to leave you here
and I won't leave without you dearest

And I'm aware that I've been distancing
to earn my place on your shelves,

in their heads, in yours hands,
with this light

Tell us one more
Show us millions for eons to come

HANDS HIGH, SMILE WIDE

I cannot wait to hold you nigh
and sing you to beddy-bye
Sweet cherubim left behind
You give me life from beyond

Mothers, fathers, you need not carry
this black and heavy pail of tears

When they hold him tight
and look into his eyes,
I can see her dancing,
shining into mine

GHOSTS OF INFINITY

You've got to do right
by your own head,
in your own hand,
for your only heart

Ghosts of infinity,
sharpen your penships,
for the crows' ink flows

Pick your precious fill
of anonymity's finest,
written in your last will to test

Meant to give your best
What on earth could ever
inspire this much and suchlike?
Such is the sign
Such a time of waste

I've got no lock and key
for your parchment
bleeding through me

I'm not opposed to trying,
not lying to myself or you,
or anyone for that matter

Just don't take me away from
your aching song for too long

It's not too heavy
to hold it up to our hearts
and learn about you truly

The way you see us
The way you see the worlds in us

To laugh and cry right next to you
Can't hold them close enough

It's open séance
It all makes frankincense
says the heathen poet

BACK FROM THE DEPTHS

Going out to the feature with friends
Taking the triptych way in
at Night Creature Park again

Saviors lurking from the dark,
in Perpetual Daydream City
Alive from those depths at nightfall

Forever never always running unbound
How long can you keep this going on?
Find that diamond beneath the surface

Death red swan bathing in the fountain,
boiling in the heat of the nightmare

The reaping sowers
run for the covers up to the neck

Here in your bed,
head is never safe from pestilence

Mental disruption
Totalitarian dereliction
Can't undo this
Anyone can be corrupted

You can do this
So overly productive

Anyone can be disruptive
Make your dark pleasantries constructive

It can all come to you as you see it,
if you let the moment breathe on its own
and get your mindset ready to go there

As it sees you,
the light will come out
to help you see the lesson through

NIHILO MAGIS

Distant hand knows nothing of time
Lunar spellbound Book of Solaris fell
from the library-green fortress of shelves

And so to whom should sever or
ever try and tame them might
better watch closely on this nightly,

For the dark hour chosen
to help set alight will fall slowly
in her eyes, another life's wonder

A life enriched by the sound of
a life in which to give and let live
Breed heeds owl's mechanical screech

Blooming plumed in the waves of
an unnamable wind out of space
with a pungent scent of madness

I descend into the mirror-black craft
Just like our walking stone,
I can't stay so steadfastly gone

Away to ancient home on foot
Ancient wisdom in the corner of
the coroner's office

Examination of my mortal coffin
with your deformed accomplice
without a moral compass

Here comes the shadow of death
in a New York breath, hello,
goodbye to your soul

Old and deeply read
paperback novelist,
bold in deep red

PACT OF BROKEN LAUGHS

A pact of broken laughs
and a one way plague to the grave
that never was meant to be this way

We'll drink from the bloodred knife
beneath the veil tonight,

Crash this rocket ship
into the man in the moon's eye,
brighter than a thousand pilot lights

In the city square,
you tear with grace and carefully

No fair, no warnings given
Fare thee well for you never listened
No, your eye did not glisten in mine

ON THE HILL

So much longing
So much distance

So full of empty hopes
Much suffering in the soil

So much for the courage imbroglio
Blind rage, panic with hemorrhages

and then…bombs…gone…
an open-air slaughterhouse

Fire away, crown of blood,
killing cowards to save face

That evil witch beneath the house,
under the couch,
where your therapist asked,
"How does it feel?"

When you know in your heart
what you saw was real
In the eyes that steal,
behind the wheels of steel and fire
Marked by boundaries that deal in flesh
A bloody mess of wire and teeth

What is it you see inside of me?
What's this stuff pouring out into the street?
Whose cat's that purring in the alley
to an old Ella scat?
Did you pick that fruit
from out of this tree, son?
What is this you have come to forbid?

ELDRITCH NIGHT TERROR

Architect of the Dark Bizarre
Released by myths begot, invocations ferment
Born of the Deep Ones' dreaming

The beck and the call
has come for us travelers

The only answer that waits for never,
beheld by the Shadow One

The beast over these ancient peaks,
a star-scraping mad,
mind's eye raping monolith

DANCE OF THE SHADOW DAMSELS

I'll be doing zee tango tonight,
out with the witless miasma of bloodflies
Do the wicked flamenco, Snake Doctor
You, so careless and unwavering, fold

Unbridled, they're all waiting by the river
Cocoons you in chrysalis, mindless eyes shutter
Bare witness the undying transformation
Dragon breath furies in the night air

I hope to see you in the aftermath
to shake your molting wings again,
do the devil's knitting and finally get your name,
    come hellfire

A HAUNT IN OUR HEARTS

Don't turn to dust before you
find that diamond
in the roughest part of town
The blood will flow
to let you know,
what's yours is not mine,
wisdom divine
You'll always have a haunt in our hearts
Immortalize us once again
I want to dance with my star tonight
Can you take me there?

Portals stream into the river,
one mountain over another
Anew, born from the ashes,
out of feverish ether dreams
expelled from nowhere,
dropped out, suspended in crucifixion
Untethered this one
transcending endless dawn
between us all
Let it go on knowing,
you are the light forever shining

NEWBORN DREAMS

There are some angels
I've been waiting to kiss

A handsome little devil dreams,
chasing rabbit tails in a cradle of wings

Lots of fuzzy hanging things
spinning, lulling safe and sound

Anything is possible
when the dream comes around

WIDOW'S WINDOW

You poison-fanged, conniving beauty
Arc of my plaguing desire,
never more so than ever before

Won't you come down from those gables,
weave them a story with eight long endings
and three thousand feeding others,
paying no mind in peace?

Try again deeper within
Anticipation came and went
Encircling all known sorrows in your hands
and it's all just diamonds and blood spatter

So far…the light…so bright…
The darkness shines dawning inside,
between the great and the grand

You'll never have to crawl to understand
the beginning and the end
and all the love within
and all that surrounds

LIONESSENCE

I would tilt the moon
and sink with you
If you don't like the cover,
tear it off and see what's important

And nothing really matters
Why now?
Why not then?

Don't pretend
Time for red
Let us begin

Less talk, more sorrow
I want to lay beneath your shadow
She's seen them fall and watches them crawl to the
yellow knife all on their own
She doesn't know why
she hears their screams

A torchbearer when no one cared
Fire inside those restless lamps' light
In the city of perpetual night, there will always be a
surprise lion in wait for a feastful
Whose lies do you now see through?

The mighty oak watches over
the hunted and the maiden
under thunderous moon

Dilation of light we used
to carve our names into

I must give you uproot
as it seems, a fitting tomb

Calling up a star-borne crone
Hell-diver staring down
the eyes of Astrea

DUE TELLINGS

One abstract idea away
from giving my entire being
One more tiny dancing star
surely won't waltz over this wall

Who will last to the end of solstice?
Who will I become next, Harvest?
They are some place where
I don't fear to tread in my head

I am the only one done
who truly understands
That Saberwolf, sweet is she

Newfound verse hound twinkling above and earthbound
    in an unfamiliar pattern,
in the shallows of skies so deep
You'll never know but you'll learn
how the brave fly in this storm we weather

EXTREME ENDEAVORS

Your life will look after you
but you must look before you
die by your own hand

Autumnal son,
the falling of the coldest winter

Over the horizon
Under the tides

I'll be your spring flower showers
until our fading summer's solstice
devours all that has now soured

I have nothing but the sorrow in
these words to keep me company

I give them to you
Do you accept?

Don't answer just yet
You must first question it

Why and for what reason
don't I crumble?
It's all in the tales of time and time again
Caught somewhere in nowhere

Deep within a dreamer, a long-lost life ago
The pleasure, the pain, anguished

Scattered days, broad to extremes
I won't be around forever,
nor these words, but
I won't go quiet and ashamed

In this bottle that
always comes back
full of sand and scorpions

Decadent with barnacles and
a single breath from
the bottomless blue

Hold that thought
and let it linger
in an oblong box for one year

See what it unlocks
from your deepest
resolution chest of empty treasuries
My life was lost
I paid the boss

Nothing's what it was
worth a year ago

You'll never know
how much I've grown

Until the next break
in the psycho circle

Wear the fire well
Let your demons wail

Dark fairytales come to light,
telling themselves

Blood in the tank
I've seen too much

Now I'm the obscene,
observant and unseen

Cannot erase them from antiquity
Must retrace, moving forward…

One between nothingness and infinity
Two independent scopes go blind

Three kinds of sight
Four of mighty horsemanship

Five alive in the morning
Six in line for the rivers of lightning

Seven heavily sealed doctrines
Eight-legged gods weaving the house

Nine circles of unwanted help
Ten command themselves forthright

Ready or not, here I am
never seen again

Always on the run, ever ready
for eleventh-hour elicitation

YELLOW JACKET

Boy, you'd better think again
It's now your time, your say
Sun fires in gunpowder fields,
plowing the meat into men

A single shogun, hanging in the gust
Dust in his wounded windpipe
When the time comes in and the tide rolls by,
you'll know just what you must do

Soaring with Icarus' hubris and
other autumnal swans in song,
over a rage of hallowing earthquakes
Mystic mistress, her endless mystery
Most unfathomable beauty is she

Vengeful vultures harvesting death domestic
The lesser wrecks of Proteus
upon the eldest shores of Aether Island

Tombs of time, hiding in minds,
they speak and plague away
Like the egg tooth of a hydra noose,
a mind turned to blunt stone
cracked open, reveals the radiance within

Bayonets of bones barricade
this den of lizard-belly'd blood drunks,
in the name of thirst and hunger
Without end, they sliver where evils dare

Silkworm suits surround their gilded spoonfuls
through the light, the silver bulletin
Turning toward Victorian morgue lore,
the ventriloquist's doll called the autopsy

And if the pact should be broke
by leaf, by hound, by totem, by sundown
Left in the open wound to tell it to the moon,
to whom all this will soon make no sense

Unbroken the witches have spoken,
out of colossal diamonds in the landfill
With wonder, they wand all their wishes,
as if to spool out the spindrifts
and the different threads between them

ALLURE OF THIS CITY

Midnight locomotive steamers
scream the steel off one so far and gone

Perchance they'll dream the dreams we read
because of what was screamed that day
and spoke to them of the Xenomorphodox ritual

Knowledge of the Kingdom of Darkness
Purgatory's lost relics and scriptures
Echoes heard both near and farby

To flag a taxi in this mess, taking ages away
Twilight on the brink of breaking

Scalped tower seats to the astral symphony
Laboratories, unnaturally disastrous
One catastrophic cacophony after the other

Whereby the outliers therein,
they all hear the sounds and they're still here,
drawing themselves in fields

LEAVE THE MAESTROS TO THEIR CRAFTS

Oh, how many moons
I've stepped into your light,
walking in your shoes
to paint myself in your likeness

TREAD

You're not the only one
who believes that
store-bought folklore

Flipping and flailing about,
gripping and failing
in the no-wake zone

It breathes
We can breathe within it
and can't breathe without it

INFRA DIG

The rabbit holes are everywhere
Everyone's everything unfolds

As rich and full as any
cave of wonders one may enter

Mindful of the way you see
and all the things you touch

As every jewel in every cup,
does have its prize and price

ROOTS ALIVE

Beast stalks across
the marsh of footsteps

Hunter of darkest discoveries,
furies circling above

Rising life from below,
hollowed in this family

Born of the fruitful
that bear the seed

Dig deep down into
the dying root and bury me

HIGHLY UNLIKE LEE

Fleeting is this time for jest
Mind your rooks on the sure side
in the waving tides with the sharks

Bleeding bone-dry like this pair of dice
The front line defends equitable charges
Burden of proof lacerated on the wire

Waiting are the shadows in the shades
Closing deals on the flying circus wheel
Moral standings under cloak and dagger

NORSE STAR

Sign of Polaris
The brightest of nightmares
Eye spied Osiris, hiding behind
Psionic lotus of Máni is lifted

Ursa sings in minor
keys of eternity's unrest
Valhalla seems a rewarding afterlife
Warriors fallen, enter unanimously divided

The steadfast kid
Immovable rune, you
Where and when to next?
My guiding rider, fly on by crisis

How many moonless years
to the other side of light?
I see you're watching over the edge
within my second sight

BROCA'S SPHERE

Endless genesis of life's violent misguidance
Revelatory crossing of rivers to exit us
I hear your echoes clear, unspoken signs
through the water in this sphere

Sensing you nigh, tensions beneath the current,
muddy and merciless misprints begot
Using my inner voice for a change,
To have a chance, I choose to make a choice

Search has run dry for land
Take a drink of this titanic oasis
Looking into you the darkness appears
Never will I look back blinded

Some wisdom is dumbfounded,
hanging in the balances
Where are you hiding the mindedness?
In lightness, vanished the spiral spirit seeker

ONE COULD SPEAK

One could stand
One could crawl

One could walk
right into nothing

The spider has come
Tell us the story

Did you sleep
on a nice cold pain pill?

Because the hems at the
boot of your denims are all torn

One could guess
One could learn

One could know for certain
and say nothing

PASSER

What is one's heart
but a star in a vault,
given a false start,
revealing one's true sparrow?

A LOVIN' MOONFUL

Barnacles of wisdom, ripping to shred
Crashing waves in double red flag
Undertower, first in the water,
not thirsty anymore

Architecture of the lie,
a force of man's stipulation
The truth is an omnipresent
force of natural science

It is within us
It is, without us, sound
Snarling its lycanthropic jaw,
ready and rearing to reveal itself

And the color thus crawls
Like the raven's tapping talons and beckoning caw,
you are the reason why
the night's so dark and longing
Still I fall for her every time she calls

MEAN TO ME/NICE TO MEET YOU

No, there's no such divinity
Therefore, no recipe for
salvation nor damnation
in this or any dimension
It was never my intention though
I'm thrilled to know how much
these words mean to you
because they're all about
how much you mean to me

The hate is subject to change me
Not to forsake, thus
must make some mistakes
To wait is too late
The time is questioning
It's later now
You're not too old or too young
You're not too proud
Don't be ashamed to say it loud
Love is what makes the world go round,
not the other way around

THE VALUE OF PERCEPTION

To bleed…
To dream…
To suffer…
To think…

To look within,
find your mantra
and transcend

SILHOUETTE

Curious to catch
a glimpse of what chimes
beyond the midnight bell

If then the legends are true,
this sound will lead me swooned
and you should be sitting there

In the shadow over the eye,
where once I saw you
clawing your way through it

WHAT PART OF ETERNAL DO YOU NOT UNDERSTAND?

We never wondered
how much time had passed

It never did
It never has

We never questioned
if this life was meant to last

We always loved
We always laughed

RECEDING ENDS

We will return
when you've turned
your sun to black

And you've burned
your world ashen

In the end of your resistance,
your clones won't even
know of your existence

TO STAY

If I could be anywhere,
at any given time,

I would spend the rest of
eternity here by your side,

but you've got places to be,
people to know

You need someone
who's willing to let you go away

A goner with wings
guiding you home

ALMALETTA

The winged one, this wild's sole dark betrothed
Born 'side the pale mountain's peak
to golden rogues of exalted beauty
Huntress drawn to mystic wisdoms of Calypso,
shining clear and true and harmonious

A great howl hello, Night Fang
Dare I let her know I see
Is this all I have to give to live?

Am I not done dying, presiding?
How could anyone live like this, Freak Eye?
Have I just left my body
into a bluesy night bird passing?

Am I at the end of a dream, Dragon?
Lost in proximal paradox land
Metamorphic optical die flying

Who is she, I to her?
Am I the supernovae paradise construct?
Am I the edge you need bleed for?

I know I'm a freakish fiend
I am Autobahn Boy,
fearless and terribly unique
Her violet waves outburst me

Like the lamp in the blackest night skyline,
enveloping, sealing this feeling
I get when she is near
Suddenly, I've become the haunted party

This much is clear as my courage
now being confronted, regardless,
fear gazes in, a blind-spotted mirror appears

I fear the opaque shape moving within it
in a pattern from a lost flying forest,
beyond the pale and empty shores
of this forgotten fortress of multitudes

Do you believe in us, Winged Soul?
Vanished in the molecular facility of
blood life and soil, crossed ovarian seas

And sown, the seed was planted,
though I mustn't take for keeping,

the hilltops ring of hell's escape
This enveloping, fiery embroidery
on the lapels of the cosmic abyss

These infinite fields of black
holding within, the colors
of my own tongue
Her gaze was like a nightmare
prancing through these colors,
the mother of rainbows' end

Will we remember tomorrow
in the black teeth of this
terrible drink of sorrows,
pressed into the arms of monsters
an unseen fulfillment
yet to be achieved by creature claw?

I'll need a distraction to make this fire dance
to place it around her navel nesting
I'll need a window of delightful opportunity

The freshest waters from her stream
Where did she find the dagger?
In the back of a bigger monster?
Head hounds the mice in their tree hollow

A canopy of winged things
into the mystery and myths
of the Ancient Freaks

The widow in the doorway open wide
Shadow upon bedlam nights
Down the hazy hallway of sleep
providing an exit, and she is the key

She is a perfect scene
A silent celluloid scream
I hope she doesn't mind
all the dreaming in my eyes

Ascending unfolding feathers
among the feast of the evening,
out of twilight's beholding wisdom

We swallowed up and spat back
into deep hell tombs
That is if a soul is even a soul at all

Then she does see me
This is real, I am still
Am I still myself?

What is she reading about?
Where is she now?
Am I dead?
Is this hell my home?
Is there no end to this undertaking?

There must be something missing
Hissing kisses tell me more of your misery
by reciting the devil's prayer

Trouble in the trenches of gargoyle stone
Cavern of crystalline blood demons,
Godspeed to her coiling

Now's my time to save her
This is why she led me here
I know now, and I will never fear
any ending drawing me in
Raven-black beauty queen of despair
Heat of eternal suffering
blanketed over the dominion gorges

Coldhearted nightingale flies
She swings with the range of
one hundred fossil trumpeters

Nightshade drape our wilderness coffin
in the kingdom of the Blades of Night

Many hells and many more
horrors to tell
No worries nor wealth
This is what sweeps me underneath

The breath of ten thousand
dead-winter dragons awakened from slumber
Still she is as I first saw her,

A shadow without shape,
walking into my darkest hours,
my deepest catacombs of
shameless cruelty hidden well

Cloak of magma flows,
draped behind the eyes of dawn
Alone below
Open sharp mind like a cat
born into the ninth life
Last one to survive

Where have all your guard dogs gone?
Why have all these angels fallen lowly?

Someone must've hit the wrong
button to the mainframe

There is a peculiar stone, and
she is so far, the jewel of a star
in heaven ripped and torn apart
Forever breaking chains
where blood and fire unleash pain

The screams of sorrows torment,
torture and lament to shreds
Tears like blades
Love like shades
Ghost of an elder sage

Did you give up your body for
a ship in the sea of uncertainty,
hanging in the balance,
questioning the silence?

Answering with violence
No one to confide in,
until it's your time to descend?
May you survive this night
lest your courage not survive you

Up to the giant task
Scale the obelisk
Don't walk past him on a blank page
Filling the think tank
Ready your nonsense

We calibrate with a head start
to a race that never ends until
you decide it's not a race at all
You make the choice

You make the calls
You take the fall
Take all the shots
Obtain all the goals
Erratic, static radio wire

Pushing every elevator button
to the top that destroys
what's left of your empire

Eyes that have witnessed death
have seen it all falter
Shattered window zone
Hidden treasures take me home

Dance me to oblivion
Waltz right into darkness turning,
cascading in white light
No shadow remains in my place
Here's to dawn on restless nights

Fluorescent ceiling flies away
The eyes of night usher me with assurance
Astrea won't leave us astray
Estranged from your birth monster
In this tomb, we are misled prey

I just don't know what to do
without the snake in the garden
Leaving the king for the vultures,
swallowing the pride
I recognize your lies unwinding
and watch the truth unfold

Lazarus' eye on Bethany, wide
and waiting for the dead to reprise,
summoning up the sickness inside
Black dove, white raven
Come you must, my darling Maven

Have you heard their stories the fires
would ignite the forest's desires?
Won't you dance with death,
dance this life away with me?

Make my skeleton home here
Would you run for the fences,
or swing from the hinges?
Heartache and hell lie in wait
in the asylum-hedgerow fringes

Give me your blood, your essence, your wildflower
Good night to the sun in my heart
A locket of screaming pain for heaven's keepsake

A nuclear requiem sleeps tonight
as the day's womb entombed the stars
No guiding guardians in the zodiac
Twilight sky, goodbye to midnight
No presence of lifelong lessons to be learned,
save for the sorrows of the new day's dreamer, beat

THE LIGHT THAT CUT THE OBSIDIAN SKY

A life in this old flame
We claimed the night
on the day of the deadline

We are learning to live long
We are at the beginning of darkness
The end is not authored

What's the hot route?
What's our destiny glowing?
Anyway the jeweled wind blows
What's this song of noisy machines,
all about the journey between?

We've no destination destined
Contemplating in cathexis
Unbreakable concentration awaiting arrival
to the spiral constellation camper

Galactic seas in cosmic imaginations
The mothers of intention,
questioning our inventions
experienced to obsession

The lines are unconnected
and the dots are all rearranged
Our journey has been disrupted
by all these uneven things

Out of tune strings in December
The odds are all against us

Asking of the who, what? When? Where? Why?
And how in the wonderful world did we get here?
Is this the tonic of afterlife?

There's a song of sorrows
I would love to drown
in sounds of someone
hurting more than I am

Why do I do these things to hurt you
by hurting myself?
A hard pill to swallow

Flier of the crestfallen, eruptions dismantle conversations
and do it all without dying

We try to hold on, fear to let go
of the kind that holds fire

Warm tech unsupported
Cold blood transfusions
Ominous iris of wires

Forged in labyrinthine laboratories,
designed in the smoldering discipline
to strike while the irons are up

You'll want to die and
burn beyond your time

Who brings the light by nightfall,
lurking in the lurch with chloroform rag dolls,
hushed and snuffed to contortions in a buxom clutch?

CHASE THE DRAGON

The world needs serpents like you
Somewhere there's a reluctant rabbit
caught in the current tides
on the turbulent river's edge

We find that most of what we really need
leaves us with only what we don't understand
Time is never what they say
What is this weight worth to date?

Most of whom you can save
Why is it always far too late
when we decide to reach out?
Inside, are we what eats us alive?

Even wise knows not why the curious had to die
Questions flying by on wings of empathy
You gave up your place in the race
to bring your rain upon the raging flames

SURROUNDING

We barbed our wires at the charging fences
Shot the cannons loose over the wall,
within the hands of mindfulness

Answering the call of the beastlings,
the sound of mysteries misheard
in that old, abandoned hell storm

And when all the stories of this haunt
no longer moan or mention me,
please remember I'm still around

I've got a place in your inspiration tank
Built upon common grounding mistakes
found a solid voice to hound about

Young or old, silver or coal,
boring or bold, you are
who you carve in your own mold

We died and cast our shadows
in the light of things to come,
surrounded by love and carried home

STARVING MARVELOUSLY

Shackles rattling
Shadows cackling
They have me now
This is happening

There are no windows
There are no bars
Only doors to perception
(paradise flies out of a jar)
Only hidden walls, Jack

Stars just don't fall out of the sky
The halls of Valhalla, they do not mourn or sigh

Fear becomes courage
Don't sanitize your insanities
You're not insensitive to humanity
Can't handle reality?
Build a fortress for your maladies

The gifted in the weakest hand
And to the polluted pulpit on which it stands

One legion with many dogs
Dismantled and dissected lab frogs
The facade of this charade
in the palm of a feral godhead

Would you trade your thoughts?
A game we play, is it not?

Master of mentalities
Disastrous reality
Chomping every bit to bitterness
Remembrance in calamity
Boldness is hold on extremities

Malice of talons cup the chalice
Drink me to the heavens
Mad is the Hatter, said the malady maker's sadness

Are we who we are
beneath our self-inflicted scars?

Fairy-tailed sister, body of water
Weapons of fortune on fire,
to fiddle with the strings of a murderess

Dark elder bow of bone struck the marrow of life
Reward for return of stolen hawk, hound, and lady
One crow to the left of the murderous scenery

Watching in the deadening daylight,
we do the raven's walk on the gangplank
Can we eat him now or should we wait?

Am I to write, writhing in martyrdom,
in a garbage heap for your amusement?
Stew in the filth of which you fear to claim?

Hawk is eyeing spider, flies wayward prey
Hunter of vultures in the valley
Dexterity left its mark on the door

Stark in the motel hallway, a single letter M
Making nonsense of nuisances
no one saw cutting out of deviations within the
framework

WIND OF LONGING

Goddess gracious philosopher
I've created a monster introvert

Near and falling apart
Claws creeping far and dark
Vaulted lockjaws flying ajar
Lungs collapsing down the stairs
A squaring off showdown with a ghost

He has my blood of brethren son
He has my name, but he'll never
take my home and my heritage

Demons crawl from my throat
My sight is set and my
compass points to nowhere
What direction may befall you
out here in witching hour?

This palace is the place
where I met my match,
burned it all to ashes
and found the beauty
rising from the unknown

Never shown the way
to get back home to the page
The children shouldn't see this
until their folks teach them
To read between the lines,
the face beneath the surf
These words are my reflection
with no worry of pretensions

You are my protection from
any fear of anyone's perception

These thoughts are just a projection
A shadow on the wall
in the shape of humility
and the color of enlightenment

(OPENS BOOK) WORLDS POUR OUT

Amulets of darkness
to color in the artist's hours
with endless mystery, stumbling
upon humble mumbled jungles

Mother earthworms, your libraries
are becoming footstools and coasters
for wise-ass fools who have no respect
for ancient tools, wisdoms, humors
They'll just let it burn and turn to dust

It all crumbles if you drink the river
Drinking memories of them away
Just lucky to have a chance at least
and though our time was cut short,
crescent lunulae did light the wake behind

Saboteurs beware, come well within
Out of the pages upon the floor
Leaning inward, beyond the door
Open-ended learning, the beholder yearns

ANTIVIDEO MAN

In the beginning, there was nothing
In the middle of something, otherworldly
In the end of everything, certain
no one can be sure of anything

Walking the path where all
straightened arrows fall in
Breathless kisses stolen,
winding in the narrows

On the wings of a wounded creature
To wander the earth in the center
of a painting of a dream
In the corner of my memory,
I saw you rising from below
Have you seen me before,
in another painting perhaps?

In a melting body of wax?
In the molting skin of a viper,
rising from the incunabula?
In the blood on the tractor,
parallaxes began ploughing their way outbound
In the arms of a devil's mother,
Like a bat out of some other dungeon

Waiting in endless night,
the ever hunting undead
Boiling heat signature, a demon fever
Pale and brazen but still a raven
My laughter is maddening
You'll never hear it in the light,
here in the arms of no one,
when the laughter turns to torture

Difficult with nothing to bite down on
No restraints to secure the itch
I can feel everything and nothing feels real
Whip-poor-will flies into eye
Cavern mouth, clenching teeth
Momentum for inertial mold warping

Ice-bone dyer's got death breath
Dyslexic wind catching this heavy feather
Anguished nimble voice like quicksand
An image engraved to memory,
burned into the bottom-feeding,
banned from the history section
The gift of losing everything
Knowing how far to get nowhere

OCULUS

Thrown to the wolverines
Out of the temple's skull alone,
go those who seek out obsessions

Ivory new moon lay dusted observatorio
Dusk, at this phase upon the sea,
bleeding she'll be crescent fluorescence

Survived through the purgatory window
because I had you, Janus,
whom I hold now in my armoire

Madness on the minded man
Bruises of the body given away,
in the womb of hidden miracles

Destroyer disturbed by their chanting
Candles light the three-legged obstacle
Atomic optic on the dotted life

Trinkets of nights alive
Twinkle little darkshines,
tinkering with time unwinding

FERMATA IN MUTA

Are we worthy enough
for your dwelling shelves?

Flying by the clockwork
of the lunar fusion bell

With no one to watch
Stories stirring themselves

We choose how we live our lives
and when the fire speaks,

Ask it and it dispels
the soprano cornucopia from a dying forest

Writer, take the time
One day we'll be leaving you behind

So put your struggle in ink,
on the page with swaying blade

In the wake of ripping waves,
wreckage of eldritch storms
Beneath the surface, we'll wait to burn
while you learn your lessons
Down the hard road, you take your turn

Set it, got it, lost and got it bad
If it burns, don't do it again
Do it again and then you might

Understand how much you can take
from this body robotic

Electric light responses
Sensitive to life but cautious
Stepping into an unconscious union

No this, without that
The one within them two

No rat without a cat
No love without that which you cast out

No doubt among the shadows
frolicking from your lips

SUMMER SIGIL

Canter of the wounded whisperer
Banter of the wickeder's persuasion

This sacred hold on
what we thought the answer

And you took the knife
back to where you found it

In the faith of the faceless,
the deviant is driven to drive

Thoughts of the heartless punk
Through the mind of the thoughtless monk

This must be the sign,
the signal significant

PILLARS OF STRENGTH

Honesty
Empathy
Diligence
Respect
Courage
Determination
Integrity
Perseverance

Pillars of strength
that stand in the face of trying times
(as the lies and the fallen test their fate)

Built upon and even stronger foundation
that is the thing we call love
So where's your answer, quest for water?
The day of night on fire, flies,
stepping to from star to star

Palladium in summer's sky
This empty thing is demolishing
my world turned to waste
In this house of gravestones,
who'll grace this eagle's landing?

You take your place in the pile
that suits your acquiescence
Everything you couldn't save,
I threw my arms around,
under our good luck charm

You deserve more than these
words of the hurt I've cursed upon you
and I don't deserve your crutch

When we wake up in the morning,
the only thing I have left is
the only thing that matters

Daggered wind they call the quiet one
Without it, there is no way in
The ancient youth do not rely on it

What makes them think so?
Why don't they speak out of their tongues,
inside the circle of celebration?

They just stare and point to the forest
with those eyes reflected *ignis fatuus*
The will o' the whip in the dead hedges

Lost art of humility
Longing for lovers of laughter
Shortness of life, never ever after

Taking turns giving nothing
Faking smiles for failure
Climbing to cosmic distances

Automatic eyes reflexive
The depth of my reflection
And then I met you

The hand that reads the mind
and plants the seed,
will surely find there is no needle

The hard way, happy and elderly
Young at heartache till the last
Pain of mind, old and purring

MY IDLE EYE

Roaming free in empty hours,
full of falling for forgiveness...

Out of the woodwork,
chopping down your door,
crawling through the floorboards,
screaming for any hell out there
Paper cut to the throat of
first and lasting impressions,
in bloom with all the blessings
you counted and surmounted
Perspective of another dream
Reality knows all too well,
his ugliness on the surface
and everywhere all at once
Not asking anyone to understand
Not above but over it all the same
If being curious is seeming crazy,
I'm curious to know why you're not

...Don't split at the first
sign of indifference

WELCOME TO BLOODTOWN

One with this battle, worn
on the sleeves of honest deeds
defending their cleverly disguising,
dangerous, and disgusting way of life
You must be proud
Olde, great, hellion hound,
it's their blood on the countryside
Their homes ran out of townships
and on your clean hands
Out of your head and heartless,
for which they stood fast
Never again will your promises
be welcome in this paradise
You must learn to see the world
through those fearful facades
to reveal the only face you need,
beneath that veil of shame
For all the lives you claimed
and the oh so many more before
Reaching acquired levels
of fame and misery, and as for the future,
for you there is only blood
Torturous suffering without end
Boy, that sure sounds like fun

GRAIN OF THOUGHT

Now you're gone, and life's
just getting older by the wayside
Don't know when I left this planet,
looking toward the sunshine

Morning raining to uprise
No buffalo to call my son
No honor for our fathers' gun

Bleeding from your intentions,
where the bullets roam
These shells you keep losing count
Smelter of shining elephant's foot
Poison treatments by radiation leakage
Component of ringing thunder
in a blazing of trail trampled tramps
Floor of flooded order has arrived

Crowing in fields of strange,
skins left behind to dyer's dust
have overstepped and taken root upon them
Desert of every wish granted,
making sure they hold up their end

All that she had left were
footprints, walking planets
No land in hand over the risk
To wander in a cautionary tale
Digging—turning—driving the mirage
into your new lost cause

Scorpio at dusk caveat
Don't trust your invisible ugliness
Circle around the bone and husk

Might not make it through the night
if these three dogs bite

For those who have chosen to stay,
this is just the tip of the ice pick
Beauties in discovery slip between the cracks,

Revealing cryonic embryos
preserved for this moment,
to uncover the distances

Equally the reason why
I can't find my left shoe,
right here just for you
in a thousand years or twelve

Are those horses in the trees
or just a regime of armed forces
forced to freeze under the cover?

Clusters of troubled trenches
Will they ever come to your senses
making a monarchy, maniacally so?

Attempts to make amends
to find out where it all begins
Might it be we'd found simultaneous ground?

When all of this ends tomorrow,
will we find out what the cosmos holds,
while every grain of thought
in the hourglass falling explodes?

HEARTHSTONE

Of precious hearthstone from the sun
The huntress of the heavens
and the hunting boy named Earth
In this one and lonely zone,
two danced in circles of vaporous films,
strolling like hellions for eons

Ninety-nine lives the desired amount
Amassing far too stellar, unpredictable
Pushing all the luck buttons and running
Forth comes the crystal island
Out of the flying circus, dragged and jagged
Swallowed alive by this cavernous classic
of the boy whose name unleashed the beast
and the huntress who haunts me,
wolfs down the eyes at night, bejeweled

Echoes of planets panting, aurally cosmic
A light less hidden in the isle,
smiling with his fossil tools
is practicing his nocturnes
Pulled from white hole rays of rainbow dust
Once upon a wisdom stuck between teeth
Dangling with his new friends

Winged things in nightmares cull
Naked skullion breasts in daydream light
There was no measure of time
No matter or atomizer, however wide
That spectrometer never did work right

More meaningless meanderings at best
I see now as I could not then
what my dreams were meant for
Where I was in the dream within
and where I am now are the same place,
only reversed and out of space
Less painful and more terrifying
Picking up the pieces, the species

A heaving helping of heathen's breath
Dropping the kids off to school
in the morning moonlight
and of the magnitude to which
they will someday decide for themselves
whatever eternities are worth
this short life's trying trials
in purgatory's twilight hanging high on ends

THE GOOD EVIL

I revel over love of this revolver's twist
Cold beneath the son of a father's gun
Holding golden hours I'd miss out on
in the witch's time of need
And watch as glass trees
obstruct every sunset
Falling asleep to the town dragonfly
Wild, this guy's unearthly disguise filled the sky

With the blood of our brethren sisters,
it is believed they bear no mark
None of which no natural would carry
or would ever dare cross or bury over hill
Magics wax the midnight air, breathless still
If you don't will it, no one will
The serrated edge of light less traveled
along the nexus point of darkness

In a halfway house on a tightrope
within an hourglass without any sand
Clockwork breaking backward
Unlocked, *et tempus fugit*
In long-term memory of perception
by my hand with no recollection stamped

Glove up for the masquerade
This heavy foot is driving home
From sweat to swinging
off the beaten path
From bad to good riddance
Redefine and reemerge ominous-like
To give is to evolve
Evil takes life unresolved, entwined light

Puzzled pacers piece peace together,
fight for freedom's redeemable pastures
A nameless land, a headless horse
Wolves in the foreground, dire
Bison briskly graze
Form of forest changes
Mountainous metamorphic features
Pleasantries of deepened dreaming

And I am very much aware
that I cannot be near them
to roam this desert island adrift
where all the straight go strangely
Death's toll, tremulous, uncharted
Silent cemetery rises with the early births

SEARCHING FOR A BULLET

I was searching for a bullet
Saw it rip through this mirror
and knew you had it in you

And for whom do I toll this hour
at the tombs tomorrow?
Bring the drum and the moon things

A step toward the stone
with the glow of marrow
Taking turns feeding the pantheon

Rattled charmers shed to size
Just look at the little devils crawling,
getting full and filled on sky

The voices in my hand,
they do the deed
We fight for each other's own

In our own obsessions,
absorptions, interpretations,
outcries

RENT TO OWN

Pause, play it backward
'Plause, pay it forward
said the lord of the store

Outside the boundaries, foundless
Between the cracks, timeless
Infinitesimal, mysterious experiences

Mind, rewind before hand
Wind, remind me after day three
Bring it back to the can, if you please

This close to giving it back
We just knew they'd never miss
CKY2K on tape…no way!

THE MIRAGE DOOR (OPENER)

Ivory-billed carpenters abandon toils, off witching
Cravings saw a way out of extinction
Someone, some faun somewhere
out there listening with intriguing eaves
with enthusiastic persistence and precision

We took a trip in a blank canvas
We drove so far, so vividly
So why'd you stop?

In the burgeoning circle, we're
nowhere near the clearing, in the forest, swung
hearing voices that rang of Virginia's coil

We slaughtered the trail
Destroyed, our choices, down to straws
The voices grew like fungal diamonds
Their cold and patternless cloisters,
stampede for the obscurity of the darkness

Now still, deafening
I'd watched you fly into the wall
You went through it all and

It was as if you'd already
known and had gone
wandering into this side of the skies

I'd never known you had this in you
Do I dare to follow footprints
into the willows' hollow home?
However, that seed did grow in my soul, this

Who will be on the other side?
Where will this pathway take me?
Will it erase the me out here?

Deep novella,
I see you've been through hell
on the way downtown
and out of healing hands,
hard at work to save my life again

It is so much easier to
please the dark side with the
eyes of a patron saint of light

Together like dreams and feathers,
rivers and rainbow tornadoes
Where do they end up?

What claims the bone dust at the bottom
at the edge of her bedside tabula,
talking in tongues, sliming through its teeth?

Dripping down to the floor lords,
seeping sandstorms, a cold knockout,
the snaggle truth falls

Old Wordy Bird, observer,
don't wait for yesterday
to become tomorrow's heavy burden

You claim the dark has shown you
And I, my best self, well on my way
to a better me today

THE MIRAGE DOOR (CLOSER)

Whether we learn more over time or less over time, the mysteries are sure to become far more complex and mysterious as time and life go on. Before and after we are gone, there is still time to unwind and to then unravel the mytho-mysterioso kind of fire. The distances which allow one to create different senses of what life can be discovered out of the curious mind into the fabric of everything you know and guess it to be so. This is no ending anyone could've seen coming from me, out of places and times when speechless and unknown in the land of indeterminate waste. There is the moment I became better than I was moments ago. Stereoscopic oasis ahead in the clear singing, "Rescue us with your mirage door." The floor is the sky in the eye of my world-turning tide. Come lay next to nothing swept away by an untitled wave. You came of age in a time when nothing would ever be here to see this, to see you turning pages, finding your ways.

A TREASURE OF A SECRET

Am I so far in the future I can't see what is happening now right in front of you? Were you born under the scope of a microcosm or something? Rocks still roll on when the going gets toughest and the tablets turn to dust and the tables turn on us in times of trouble when the cellular tower turns to rubble. This is all that's left. And so the rock adapts and keeps on rolling with the river's flow. Even so, I'll remember who I am. This'll have to do. That'll show 'em. I will always write what's troubling my mind, wrestling with my heart, pulling me down with insecurities, and all misunderstandings will be further unexplained through the lens you might find along the way. Marked on the page was the time we shared in the tunnel where our visions were sent to the other side of this stage in our lives. We will always have that night, but we'll never always have the time.

THE LEARNING OF MEANING

Looking further on, Celesteon
past flesh of train wreck
It's not only the one,
there's still living down under

Swimming inside beast of mind,
connected to it all sometimes

Bottles in faction science jars,
plaguing me like a disease
You gave me the dizzies, dear darling

And only just begun
I'm just getting ready,
for you've given this your sole life

There's too much here to die for now
So we take the hard road

On the way to the path inward,
outside the lining

You make no mistake
that you erase from memory

All you now live for,
every wonderful time
will have its life after risk

Guide my hand with your graciousness
and your questioning why

Never sleeping soundless,
the nesting raven's curtain-black wings

Watching, waning on me,
driving the dropper's dripper homeless
Master's always known bestial unrest

ACTION

Watching over, waking in strange worlds, forming closest friendships, circling vivid stories by the fire in the waterwheel. The dreadful hours. The morning poetry with breakfast. No separation from fear and anxiety to patience and the reality of surviving this night without a fighting force. Never knowing you knew the way. You've never been this far out or this clever. The trail trickles off at the fork in the causeway lane. Words remain in question and the answer to "what was the big deal?" The real thing. Give us the entire story in detail. Like Socrates' teachings tell, it's all in how you experience, what you act upon.

To dream and to execute the thing for no other purpose or reason but to save yourself and to know that nothing is impossible when you're doing what you love. And that passion might, quite possibly, hopefully inspire someone. If only you should be the sole heir of these words and give you strength to keep going and growing. We can get through this. Out of this mess together—humble at best. Never settling for lesser than last in line for a life without the life you give me. First in line for fire and death, blood and respect, laughter and honesty in the worst of times. You were there for all of it. The greatest respect I have in my heart is for you and you alone. No one else can take the place of you. I'm learning to see through your eyes and feel around for what I'd lost sight of somewhere in time.

When we were out of our minds and losing the most beautiful companionship that almost paid the greatest price. Now is where you are not alone, and I can no longer take that for granted as long as I've lived. There was a time when I didn't know where to find you. I couldn't have been more wrong about you then, but now, I can always find the way to reach out. Here, in this story, I've made for you and for them.

REFLECTION IN THE DIRT

I once recall a reflection in the dirt,
mudding waters of all I stood for

Every loved one spoken for,
I no longer speak to anymore

Lest I ever forget you, amid the oddity
out of the blue dawning

A change in you becomes
a chance to be able to be at ease
I know it's what you want deep down
I want it for myself as welcomed

I'll always be within reach,
no matter how far life
takes us away from each other

There's never a time that I don't
wish you were by my side

My happy thoughts are you
They work like decadent charmers

Never straying too far from where
we are at any moment given

Your shoulders hold my deepest sorrows
Your ears have heard my ugliest words
that hurt the most when spat at you

At the time,
it was what it is now, behind us
as the pain that once was

And could no longer come between us
The anger that came out was beneath me

I'll always remember your empathy
and your true nature second

First and most of all,
your hand in mine

TIME OF THE SIGNS

These new dead-reds jab brains, Jack
Awake in the head
Head beats hard, bets on black
and your handle on this candle's
dark, flickering star,
breaks apart with this
silhouette of enlightenment,
solely in this shadow in shambles

Flashing horizon horses hoof it and
get on every setting of every strangely familiar sun
when I knew everything and nothing made sense
Done with all I've made since the accident,
accepting of the unexpected
Harvesting the knowledge of
my unknowing stupidity
Leave us to the greenhouses

Mind racing, I sometimes find myself pacing
so fast I can taste the smelter's edge
of yesterday's hell on my tongue
Chasing my own tales of thorns
in the haunt that built the madman

Tales of old and the new you
Trails of ice dusted, picked up
Vaporize the nucleus of suffering

with imaginations spread far wider
Rarer beauty to be born
and to die
in its sight, in light of things to come,
in spite of all that came and went
since your last visitation

As time leaps steadily without hesitation,
one cannot deny with too many
witnesses and testimonials,
the worst is yet to happen, and
the best is said to come undone

I am becoming what was no one,
and I'm still not nothing yet
and will not rest until body of work
passes by like the comet closing inward
Getting closer every year and four score
In another forty more, we'll get to
see him for certain, I hope sure

THERE SO YOU CAN ALWAYS GO

There so you can always go
and that you might understand
the way I saw the words
In case you never knew then, the way
I see you now in my obscured world
When it went down on paperback,
lifts my head up the longer
I learn and live a little lighter
than I used to choose to die for
anything without seeing the big picture
A much bolder, broader portraiture
by the shadow swimming in the sea's fire
To have and to hold one's own
Living up to this tree planted
from the seed sure to outgrow me
Stronger than I'll ever live to see firsthand
in the garden of eternal resting players
Pay with fleeting moments
Present and cautiously stealing
precious golden yearlings
All that stays when the ghost is near
What is this I fear before me?

GOLDEN EAGLE WHOSE HEART ACHED OF THAT WHICH HIS HEAD WAS BURIED SO DEEPLY WITHIN

Time and chime against the wind,
I turn it on, and then it starts
tearing me to pieces,
apart from the outside, the end all

I know nothing when I see it
Do you, too, see everything as it is?
Infinity? Oneness? Every ware between?

When I put my evil
thoughts behind me,
I find much to look
ahead for a change

Even though sometimes,
it's just not enough
So strangely, so tough

Uncharted and rough around the edge
In the center of it all,
the bursting egg births
the yolk of the ego

Too close, so far away
Closed off from those
moments out of time and players
Place your hand that reads aloud
Cannot erase, but you can hold it
if you don't look it in the eye ahead

Take one and pass them back and
don't forget to leave your mark on them
so we can trace it
and replace you with this new machine
Smooth, swift, clean, no mistakes,
no accidents, no questions,
only answers without problems or
indiscretions, interruption

No dream of a better life
or any life at any cost
No care of worry,
anxieties, insecurities, intrigues
The need is here
and the want is not always clear
Upon first glance, once ignited,
come the fires to light

KIDIOTS, OR ELDERS OF THE THIRD MILLENNIUM

In the worst possible moment
and for no reasonable why,
outpours of poisonous blood spreading
overpopulate the party line
Slithering from pastures afire,
recoiled from hoof under hood
A hissing spinster with diamonds
like the spurred heels of a jackboot

Crosses overtly the line, beckons
the sixth to sign in at the template,
leaving the Starbuck horse
to take the seventh beyond the thresholder

A great river in a dreaming world
A new meadow for the children
with the eyes of animalia
rising up to take their place
among the herd of strays

Begins anew, the journey
Come to passionate enthusiasm,
classically untraceable

All them ole trippers,
new monkey business tricks

scraping awake their crow's feet
We have a laugh about it now, then
something remarkable happens
We make light of times
we'd cried all the night's befalling grief
Singing our favorite songs
to all the moonless mothers,
together in each other's arms

Until we've slipped into our dreaming again
While the reality plagues,
out come this kingdom's keys to the happiness axis
An onslaught of hindsight
lost to the wilderness
in a sea of afterthought
Solutions stare before us
with the death trap built in

Pages nameless, shapely
to the unmarked masque charade
Fear conquered forms new waves
like the way of the pathless traveler,
seeming still and unfulfilled,
seamlessly forging ahead

OSMOSIS IN THE SAP & BELLONA, THE CROWS

Now, as you have unconnected
the body's building, rationed its
existential emotional resistance,

A stone once a throne to a crow,
flung from the house of learning on the fly

For no life at sleep to wake the call girls,
now lead the way, your own way,
beyond the walls to hang

Make your dreams come death
Take the seventh creation of light to its octave
Frightened flight of chances
Heartache in common displacement,
second in nature to the race winner

Despite my capacity
to mine my own mind,
poor little third party dwindles

Sometimes there are no lines to read between
No, this will not do
This cannot be done, Bellona

To the thing I have most
when I am alone, alongside her windings
A gush of river dust, clouds
vision, invisible until forgiven

For dragging us through your
invincible inventions made of mud
and rusted immovable parts
She made a rebellion without flaws
and gave you my questions
without a costume

What is life without a lesson?
What of love without forgiveness?
A death worth living for certain
words worth giving up to move forward

Take mark at grave
It's a prison celebration,
one for the fences
When swinging for the heads,
make your way quickly dying
toward the exits to the tents in the city's cape

Signs, symbols that don't connect us
will soon regret the decision to forget
where the others stand against the wall

And it's back to your hell again
Now all that's left to kill is deadliest
History shows us through the cracks,
a fragmented solution

Where do the pieces go?
Where will the lines blur when all
hidden boundaries get pushed around,
pressed just a little nudge further?

This is where the peaceless go
Kingdom done up in raven's cloak motifs,
set the communion bowie free

What is to come of the lion
once the sons have gone and the sky and the mountains
 fall?

I've opted out for the long road ahead,
in the hoax so high hoped
Expectations as low as low has ever known

To go where you
no longer whole,
no matter now

This is how you happened then,
when I let the weirdness out again
Beyond your wildest bewilderment,
the distance is why I keep digging,
going so far and wide

Too bizarrely for the old guardians to guide
Through these unexplored paths,
a fresh perspective I choose
I refuse to hide the light
where I know you won't find it

Can you find what is not hidden?
I don't believe I don't belong here,
and I refuse to believe I'm in the wrong

Here are my credentials,
well within my reflection to speak of
Never asked for, never given
All new admittance gave in
Next decision and decidedly so, you
don't need permission to live up to it

PEEPHOLE PERSON

Bus is leaving, prying passengers' eyes calling to us
Who's going to say grace
with bigger words and dark world pools?
Between turn and key, it gets wilder
We awaken on this nightly destination
where distance fell far away
and night closed her eye to die with dignity
To divinity, some prayed openly
for the rain to bring violent rays

The bus never did come,
but Saturday did as it dawned
on the peephole people, squinting in
Into damaged head, set careless eyes
Shuffle back to the dimmed shelters of
the big cat's cavern who seldom dwell
alone as one can go by neurocraft

Flung-off robes, uncloaked smoker,
dancing the cold away naked and frayed
In this age of ending silence,
voices in my hands paid in fool's gold
At the foot of his demise,
there's no one left to help you
I can spy your name in darkness,
the phony kill booth, the cathedral wires
Clock at work, time at hand to stone

and don't feel lonesome or loss
Trickle little icicle, feel what you will
I'm a lunar dream on a lucid stream
At night I fly until I get tired,
pick apart what fires are dying

Every clown in this town is a
beast crooned and soothed by a muse,
stumbling into the eye of this blackest night
Should've seen her go on sown into seed, zoned in on
Electric ladies and gentle giants
Thunder bolt surgeries quake the earthbound,
restlessly contempt on driving it home
Silence like a hurricane, hushed lulls gushing

Gift of the golden hand, priceless eye sickle
She spoke with voluminous knowledge,
dripping hair down to her firebed gems,
calling for a lover's spread
At the green light with magnifying lenses
for one to zero in on end

AN OLD PAIR OF VOICES ON DAMNATION STREET IN THE CITY OF SHARED DESPAIR FOR THE PRICE OF A LOST TIME

With more of the goings-on still to come
And so as the soothsayer says to me,
smooth sailing to all you undead
Minds with longer lives flashing never panned

Damnation, it's time we opened up shop
Beautiful realizations from the tree,
undershot the bloody conveyer belt
around the times you bled in drooling

Home to us, safe and doubtfully sound
and in the taxicab graveyard procession,
pentatonic back-away allies blues on by
Fellatio in exchange for his pseudoscience

They listen to me here, and there's a hole
in the place where makers meet
the fates and rise ready the fight above
Casting of shadows over the harvest

At the bridge, where 'til now, no one knew
Grapefruit wheels a-turnin', ripen with wrought
I don't feel so lost as I let ring my heavy thoughts
Monster, I've created you to become this

Look and observe what they see
Temperatures clambering up to the temple
Do you want the same love?
Day trip to Saturn or San Francisco

Of lying to myself, I put you in words
Dying on the day of frowning
Upside down but I'm saber-toothed
The somber before closing time

Free to come for blood and nothing else,
toward the open season of the eyes
Aversion's a-go in the studio, lightning lifts her veil
in the shallow's end with the unlearned

Like ultraviolet waves raised,
trick of the tale by puppeteer
How will you wake your dead?
I thought you said you would if you could
The moment laid to rest, nevertheless
Hell would reign unfrozen and sanctioned by the
exact moment when the whole thing backfires,
trips wire, combusts one's self awareness

THE HEAVENS BEFORE US

Any moment now, beneath his hopeless breath,
head bowed, kneels at the prayer's bed

Only thing louder than silence is the night
Mouthed and mimed, your mannerisms

Alone is no safe haven
Sun beckons us over, uneasy on the eyes

Spent wasting the pain away
Put down, bark back, all out of push to start
with this aftermath problem in the hourglass

I've got to hand it to you, child,
you are one most desperate man
Suicide missionaries in the unclassified

Show him where to stand and face them
Hands clasp in curse, laughter cracks backward,

Ascends into its waiting darkness
and breaks their son's earthly inventions

Moon fall undercover of endless blooms
Mind your turbines,
turbulence trembling at your feet

A place of my own in sacred space
Completely honest with me, but it takes
some others a little more

Topless fountain of Elder's Isle
Someone still wants to keep you around

In this cell, met with judgment, solidarity,
the only one who's laughing song did swoon

Midsummer sanitarium rings an out of tune nocturne
A sunburned bluebird's off-beat-scat-box-minuet

Free to roam, free to eat at home
No one ever saw her coming

From the never-ending sea of suns
in your mind, your will to find

Changes make new changes
and hypocrisy was swallowed at last

Over the heads of every theater of mind,
betwixt the skeletal facsimile of life

Fearless, not afraid of anything eldritch
Surely mistaken as absolute or the lesser

Never will you witness hope, they said,
or take place among the pillarheads

In the light of the lost and forsaken,
Earth and Mother make lovesblood

Root of all that has stayed hidden, embedded
Engravings, cosmic glyphs shone for eons over

THE SUMMONER

To you, Ladylord of this triumphant land,
who knew it, the moment I lit the fuse
Lost in suturing the pieces found

Not the same as nothing out here is
No one left to peel their way through life

Some day's sun comes up again,
you turn my attention to listen
Watch the buzzards circumnavigate like barflies
How many, how cruel, she?
And I help them follow through

Everything worth nothing,
stolen with every intention to send help

Light facing forth the path of the sleeping
Supernova eye on the priceless

I do mind, I've not forgotten what it takes
Imagine no imagination—go on then

Do this impossible thing
evolved to then project progress

Pluck the crow's feather from your brow
Share the quality of life worth living

On this trail of dead, lakeside
This hell on wings unto itself will arise

The wizard's solution in the question
Mysterious man on the move

Soon the tune begins to eat alone
in the middle of the universe

Some other, I'd hoped for evermore
Night burns brightly behind

You are in the presence of your genius
The elements dance out of their element

This is not the place you call
every promise made, every word given

No man waits for tomorrow to discover
Shrines in the stars, bright in this knife light

What is this language, coming across
monstrous and mad with evil?

Never will be your ever truly
of the one we called, Pain

To the death grove of leaves,
of neglect—sheer abandonment

Makes us weak and strengthens
to do all that we must do to protect

our children's world from within
As if they see what's coming

Account for every doubt and whim
The days you missed to take off

Mothers taught us, sow well for the reaper,
cursed with these gifts

Who's keeping the teeth of all oddities orbital within?

The insider's outcries open up
Good night to your cornerstone street curb

Intentions of those conducting
carry out the feed to needy

For a token moment of crooked trust
none would have intended to send

A shot in darkness turning loose
My chosen jewel, and I locked on

The trigger won't feel the weight
Let it take my self instead

Give what is missing to the head
It's your word over theirs

Absorb, interpret internally
Eyelids leave a trail in the vapors

A nameless ode to ideals
Tears burn, boiling over nothing
have been bewitched again

By a scorcher of rays feasting
on misery mile, nickel for a time

To whisper under the monolith in his dreams
of the stone house they make and monopolize

She was everything but set and funny enough,
a precious gem from no man's mountain

Many times and many worlds over,
the landscape of musical arrangements

When it's time to change, go changed,
transcribed and never spoken

The protruding discipline of other mothers
Sky below, earth between

To speak of in our new language
of the childlike minds we enrich

Forgotten I will begin to enjoy
Pain and poisons to balance the gimbal

The infinite springing of trees
At the same moment, body and phases sign off

Rise free from their world views
I wish to speak to you alone

The days missed to take away
from the final argument

Tell them what you showed me
so we don't seem to be the only thing

Letting loose ends get to shore
Solar call for code of man

When you're ready, my angel
Lamplight dim above the test

Conducting the results in this letter,
the truth never outweighs the lies

Players pay in full view
of their message to the world

Fallen from the heathen's gun
Mind opens the golden box

Taking this heavy handed,
gives you all the riches, the books

Demonstration of something which
seems to cut right through instinctively

Scale of sliming trails leading up to
the road of a nameless oath
Somber mood between moons

We won't skip over your song
these children left unscathed

Infinite, universal to make
this house of carcasses a home

She was uncertain of the sunset
I've got enough to get to the next life

I have witnessed greatness in chaos,
put it all together to see if it fits
Wake up, dream's over, make up

This life, this reel, it never ends
Choking on globs of child undercooked

The golden goose, a mysterious bird book
Today is this way
Haven't you learned?

New dawn's angels fly for you tonight
as you bury your dread alive

Body and mind collide to make light
Promises misfire, break like twigs

Never having to leave entirely
Given and taken by the light

ZERO TO ZERO

The power to say no even though
of this pastured lifetime, so many unknowns
Nobody wins in the end of its cycle
No need to waste the breath that couldn't save

It's only just the three faceless horsemen
questioning every fly following our vapor tail
All the more reason to hang it up,
Nest of the confessional persuasion

Might've I been misread
by the pendulum and another
one reflected back at them

The voice is yours to choose
from the dream you keep inside
Finger on the pressing impulse

Albums and instruments and tools
having a lasting impression

Message sent to the wrong address
from one's entire being
at the top of the hissing tree

An aimless arrow sees no error in its way
We won't miss a beat, our songs in tongue
Everything in its wake, it shook us
Just watch and you wait with truth

Take it slow, make it last
She sees positive emotion in you, son
in many forms in any place within

Caution: conscious of confidence
A new dream you make believe

Begins with their one and only wisdom
which can only be explained this way
Repelled from this life to a deserted palace

No deathless wonder or parasitic word
ever goes away completely in the shadow of us all

Given the tools to craft,
spirits travel parallel plains of sight
forming volcanic inner visions

ARE YOU ALONE? ARE YOU ALONE?

Once again, upon waking from an imminent death,
    the answer's continue to question
Always of another unearthly sign between

Are you listening from the tonic?
What's it going to take to get through you?

It's them or me, and I can't yet
watch in bewilderment,
o'er sand and sea and canyon

There's a light out there somewhere, glistening in
    darkness
None were ever good enough, leave 'em

Hard to take, surrealistically shaken
A double agent, triple the payment
only to be trampled upon
and under its sway,
swinging over its prey,
against the bloodstained glass in these sawed-off halves

How you talk and how you walk
through the heaviest hidden forests

One revolving nightmare of enlightened delusion
    after the next

Time will spill, even if the clocks say otherwise

We need someone like you
to make it so that anyone can see,

Pouring with impassioned speech,
haunting its prayers
It wants you instead to stay
Get ready to hold your breath,
leaping to our destination

None? You've gotta have one
This special space is mine

In desperate need of action
You may not have noticed
I've cut the seam,

The right line at the end scene
And as for their faith in the dream,
it is not customary to swirl

This world, new to you and a few
I shouldn't have abandoned
in times of fortitude

What looks up must look onward
With my ideas, I'll set myself free
to the end of my existence and further still

Leaving home and loved ones
in scattered patterns piling up in the garden overgrown

CREATION AND MYTHS

Crumbled to bits with one simple gifted wish
to speak to them of loneliness

Away from thistles, my final argumentative
Tell them what you told me, my darkest
Let them loose upon solar shores

Soldiers call for the code names
Whenever you're ready, my waxen angel guarding

Tests result in this Rorschach calligraphic
Kerosene lamplight dimming above
the word of messengers in the dead-world pool

Rain fallen from the heathen's gun
Eye opens golden box with trodden edges

Weight of this heavy-handed anchorage
gives you all the riches, the books

A demonstrational tapestry of deceit
which seems to cut right through

Instinctively with one's third party,
sliming scales lead up to the turning

The road to a nameless lake o' lights
By the scorched earth flames, we feast

Dawn is coming for us, the infinitely universal
nights uncertain in the mechanical sense

Chiming children in a windless wilderness
Lives of learning, lessons of legends adrift
Creatures cultured with creation and myths
Angels fall for you, this nightly itch,
should they carry your dread

Pendulum swings of honest toil to a trembling thread
It is not the day that waits for Death

Whereby, tomb stars align with naked eye,
blurring the lines in the slurs of blank, crowded
minds

REVELATION DAYS

Instruments of warriors scream raw emotion out of tune
Odd time intrigues, oft' nightmaresque, creeping out
Siren arise in the songbird's spirit burning, ringing free
Shot in the eye of dawn, this apocalypse blood storm

ACKNOWLEDGMENTS

A special thanks to everyone at Fulton Books for their passion, hard work, and dedication to making this book the best it can be.

An extra special thanks to my friends and family for their undying love, support, and inspiration.

Everything I write comes from something that came before. These are some of the writers that have inspired my work throughout the years: Edgar Allan Poe, William S. Burroughs, Allen Ginsberg, Jack Kerouac, Arthur Rimbaud, Max Jacob, Jean Cocteau, Sylvia Plath, Hunter S. Thompson, Charles Bukowski, H. P. Lovecraft, Bram Stoker, Clive Barker, Julio Cortázar, Margaret Mitchell, William Blake, Herman Melville, Robert Louis Stevenson, Carlo Collodi, Max Brand, Alistair MacLean, Walt Whitman, Ernest Hemingway, E. E. Cummings, Carl Michael Bellman, Leonard Cohen, Nick Cave, Jim Morrison, Bob Dylan, Patti Smith, Neil Peart, Bruce Dickinson, Julian Doyle, Stephen King, Neil Gaiman, Frank Herbert, Friedrich Nietzsche, Plato, Aristotle, Homer, Pyrrho, Miguel de Cervantes, Ayn Rand, Aldus Huxley, Philip K. Dick, Chuck Palahniuk, Henry David Thoreau, Dante Alighieri, Elizabeth Redfern, Hermann Hesse, Lewis Carroll, Walter Scott, Alfred Tennyson, Brian Rihlmann.

ABOUT THE AUTHOR

Cody Grinslade is a writer from Florida who began writing poetry in 2005 and has released (as Dakota Grinslade) two self-published poetry books: *Thorned Tales and Other Maddening Haunts* (2019) and *When the Skin Tears* (2021).

Having no formal training in creative writing, my passion for words and language is what drives me, as well as a desire to better understand the psychology of human behavior by looking inward.

My other hobbies include reading, listening to vinyl, playing bass/guitar, and skateboarding.

www.ingramcontent.com/pod-product-compliance
Lightning Source LLC
Chambersburg PA
CBHW021922030225
21333CB00040B/307
9798889828877